THE GEEZ

ALSO BY NII AYIKWEI PARKES

Poetry
eyes of a boy, lips of a man
M is for Madrigal
Ballast
The Makings of You

Fiction
Tail of the Blue Bird

For Children
Tales from Africa

As Editor
Tell Tales: Volume 3
Dance the Guns to Silence: 100 Poems for Ken Saro-Wiwa
X-24 unclassified: a ccollection of short stories
South of South
Filigree

THE GEEZ

POEMS

NII AYIKWEI PARKES

P E E P A L   T R E E

First published in Great Britain in 2020
Peepal Tree Press Ltd
17 King's Avenue
Leeds LS6 1QS
UK

ISBN 13: 9781845234775

Supported using public funding by
ARTS COUNCIL
ENGLAND

CONTENTS

GAME

OF LANGUAGE

It might have been one night celebrating
a mother's birthday in a Paris hotel room,
or some breathless minutes at the in-laws'
whispering like experimenting teenagers – still,
out of the fifty-thousand scent memory we have

there is now the smell of a baby girl, one born

in a war zone less equipped than Syria
but, for a child at the front lines, perhaps
just as damaging as time unravels. You are
her father; she is a cheeky, fragile joy,

but, because you love her, you must leave.

A coin tosses endlessly in your head; sleepless
nights have your heart torn and off-kilter.
You wrestle your selfish urges, find strength
to walk away. You know it is right,

but you have never known pain like this

and how can a suckling baby understand why
a shadow inhabits the space that was her
father? Except, your first time alone with her,
after she has left her mother's arms, she holds
you, doesn't.let.go, for the longest time.

OFFSIDE

Because I know about green mangoes
more than I know about any woman,
I teach my sister about boys, how to

think like one, play one step ahead.
I tell her not to step back any time
they lunge forward, but to side-step,

stay focused, show no fear. I show her
the same thing works in football, how before
the age of positions, they rush like dogs;

that's when you pass and move, hold on
for a minute, then accelerate. Speed
combined with timing, like a good joke,

and you have beaten the offside trap.
I teach her to punch, too, and, for good
measure, where. By sixteen, maths is play

for her; she has boys rapt for her punch
lines, waiting, hoping for a chance to slip
a line of their own in. She foils them

all. Years later when she has settled,
done her 38 weeks, I get the call. I am told,
It's a boy. It's a boy, it's a boy, it's a boy!

SEEING EYES

Pretending I can't find my bi yoo bibioo
simply because she has covered her eyes
gives her as much joy as the silly faces
I sometimes pull. Out of the 43 facial muscles
I should have, I stretch, contract, contort,

conjure shapes that get the desired reaction.

But when she hides, *she* is in control – even
ridicules me for not seeing her: *I'm right
here, Daddy*, she screams, then runs to hug me.
Already the time is coming when the trick will be

too old. I know so well how soon our pleasures go.

I recall hiding from my grandma. Her dark eyes
imprisoned behind cataracts, I was always stunned
how easily she found me. She didn't even move;
she just pointed, and my reaction was always – *How?*

Some quality of those hours with her is how I see God:

something of her certainty that I had my late father's
physiognomy just from the sound of my voice; how
she hugged this inherited body, this borrowed
shape and hue, close to her, cradled its shifting
face, seeing and loving a grandchild – with no eyes.

FRANKENSTEIN

You know that Kareem Abdul Jabbar hook
shot, right? Drexler's glide, Pippen knocking
the ball away from someone's control to send it
up to Air… Something you could always count on
when things got rough. That was Victor for us;

the opponent's worst enemy. He came on
when games got tight, when pushing, shoving
and trash talk started to creep into the game
plan. We knew the secret; he only played
well when angry. They'd make their own monster.

The more they pushed, the sweeter the song
of his bounce; the harder they shoved, the surer
his aim became, his balance impeccable as he let
his shooting-hand hang limp after each projectile
took flight. He had something we all didn't; he knew

gravity was a kind of violence too; you had to ride it.
They just reminded him of his father – a short man
who had shredded his mother with his sharp tongue,
slapped his son until the day his six-foot-six seed snapped,
grabbed him by the neck the same way he plucked

a rebound out of the air. We thought Victor was freak
material – a unique beast – until we saw his sister play.
She was good all the time – every quarter of the clock
face – moved like a whispered insult, precise as a second
hand, her fury constant as the force that held us down.

VARIABLES
(a gambil)

Asked about heartbreak, X might drop
a matchstick and raise a finger to point
at a delivery van rolling heavily past
a home. Let's say it's blue as a flame's heart
and it stops in front of a brick building

where, on the third floor, a boy (Y) is framed

in his window perch by the yellow lamp-
light beyond him. Y has headphones like planets
over his ears and is bent over a sheet
of paper, shading blackness into faces.

The window next to his is an animation;

two adult figures gesturing, their mouths black holes.
Because of the galaxy he carries, the window
boy – Y – will not hear his parents' battle, but
high above the van's blue, a beat is breaking.

X has not said a word, weary gaze focused
outside. The match X dropped will grow
into a fire X won't notice but for its heat,
won't recognise – for who would call a window
a mirror? Has no one ever told you heartbreak
is always elsewhere? What is Y in the world of Xs?

A GIMBAL OF BLACKNESS
for Pops

Night cannot grasp the swift flight
of wind, but blackens every tree
the air moves, paints them darker, pushes
them against the light, the shapeless
light that gives them shape to shift

before my eyes. I am often in the embrace

of night; I am myself a dark thing –
the kind that was once called boy when man –
that was born of a woman descended from hills
and a man delivered from boyhood by the sea,

a man now lifeless though he gave me life.

I am often in the embrace of dark thoughts,
in the dim grasp of memory, a bottle in hand,
reflecting the light of the moon. I recall
a can of Guinness left in a London fridge –

one my father bought but didn't get to drink –

kept for me by a well-meaning aunt. And how
hard my throat shrank with every sip, how sharp
that smooth black liquid felt inside me, how hard
these nights that blacken me, broken with grief
for a man I loved, who can no longer grieve.

HANGMAN

Out of the benign madness of our homes, we are
players of a different ilk, dreamers with no respect
for height, for flight, for the choke-hold of night.

Round midnight, when the faded lip of the rim still
gleams from the desperate reach of a weak street lamp,
like a vaselined smile beckoning in the corner of a club,

we shoot our shots and indulge in wordplay, lines
drafted onto paper each time a letter is called out –
like a basketball, nerveless despite its perpetual goosebumps,

kisses the hoop and slides in. Our Hangman is different.
We have sheaves of thick blank paper and pencils in three grades.
We're all artists. When we guess a wrong letter we draw curves

instead of lines and, because we like to fly, birds are
our thing. We call our game Wingman. As we play, feathers
emerge carrying streamlined bodies, the arcs of our three-pointers

truer with each attempt. We quote Rakim lines as the purest
form of trash talk, holding both pencil and ball like a grudge
although we're drawing the same bird. Whether we end up

with an eagle or a crow, we know there is no noose,
no pain, just the net and our dreams. Nobody dies,
even if one soars.

BALLADE FOR WESTED GIRLS WHO
WANT THE RAINBOW

Wested girl, your city has taught you to hate
the kind of men you fall for. Pictures of them
flash on local news cycles every night
when newsreaders' lips are twisted by crime
into shapes never full glass but coloured stem.
Pale news tongues never mention the melting of shea
butter in dark male hands, fingers in grandmothers' hair,

the posters of Paddington Bear that they haven't
removed from their walls since the age of seven,
how they hum love songs off-key, the nails they bite
when nervous. They've debated the shots of Sembene
Ousmane & Kurosawa, read the words of Giovanni & Auden,

played around with fistfuls of chopped coriander
to render simple meals great, but the papers
won't mention those things. Those headlines you get
that label boys as men and men as boys and

boys as scourges, mark them out as threats
by sly leans of language. You know that's truth bent,
you've seen these men's tears, but come crunch time
you still see what you've been taught, what you desire:
their bodies – those vessels with shades of darker
for skin – with muscle, with muscle, with muscle within;
with muscle, with muscle, with muscle and sin...

and you forget the epicardium, its sublayers,
the spaces it cradles within, its pockets of fear.

OF SERENDIPITY

Cybernetic serendipity was a phrase invented
for me by my father – an easy source
of laughs when a child can't shape his
soft Cs or Rs properly, but a priceless gift
for his vocabulary. Later, he would explain

gyroscopes as objects with a steady core,

their orientation maintained with the help
of outer gimbals that spin. I never asked
what happens if gimbals break, if
a heart's constant tread is unbalanced

by a break in the body that holds it;

what happens when serendipity dictates
that cancer is a hammer that knocks
gimbals out of shape? What I know
is: I was out delivering newspapers;

the weather was icy as death; I felt

my father depart at the traffic light;
I raised my handlebars and tried
to force my way through the red to my own
demise; horns blared like a final chorus
but my unbroken gyroscope stayed true.

TRUMPET

The first time you blow
a tight-lipped buzz into the funnel
of a silvered mouthpiece, you understand
Charles's Law – the one on held pressure,

not Mingus's well-thumbed message
of exact timing – that tells us all we need
to know about temperature and what volume
it moves. If it's hot, it's straight up

physics – volume is maximal. You knew,
but now you really know the fire
it takes to set that horn alight,
spark music along its burnished length,

the molten brass opening out
to spew
a resonant shaft
of burnished, burning air.

ONE NIGHT WE HOLD

for Ms Bones

One night we hold and the lights go
out. Everything in the world turns peripheral
vision. We lose ourselves in the dark edges
that pattern the wings of some bright butterfly flitting
between your skin and mine. We let go of logic,

history; we believe we are beyond the grasp of gravity,

floating as we are in these sensations we kiss
with. Time, family and friends swim
outside the urgency of our hunger. We believe
in the everlasting of love, never stopping

to wonder where we might drop anchor. We abandon

reality's compass at the border of our lips. All we know
now is the spin of intoxication, a cocktail of sighs pitched
into a cauldron of dancing flames. We carry our own light
birthed, like campfires, from friction;

two bodies moved by hands to the melting point of sodium.

We are salt separating into its elements, we are Lot's nameless
wife reclaiming our story. If nobody else looked back,
everything is a rumour. We are sweat without words;
how it feels is a held breath. Tomorrow's story sits in
the depth of our eyes, limpid as lakes reflecting night.

EROS

BOTTLE

I think of the room, the way
      it separated into definite things
in new light: the sparse spread
      of furniture; the writing table
a chequerboard of thought, schemes;
      the bed no longer neat,

      and beside
it, shiny glasses, unused, a bottle empty
      of rum, on my tongue the dance of her
sweat and the sugarcane's trapped burn
      stripped
from every limb her body possesses.

      A story —
some old pub nugget of Ethiopian women
      and their skill at splitting chickens
into twelve parts, with no need for knives,
      just a tender feel for the limits of flesh —
the fear it must inspire in stray husbands —

      comes to mind
when I imagine her body
      that morning: the hunger that tensed my being,
how I was afraid to tell her I might be
      in love with her,
      terrified

of seeding hopes
      I could not suckle,
the salt-charged taste of her,
      rum
that smoulders still
      in the back of my throat.

BREAK/ABLE

Last night we left the blinds half/open, so
the sun would wake us. The train you must catch
more important than our week/long jive

with the natural order of things. This is how it comes
to be that I witness the darkness relaxing its hold
on our bodies, yielding us to form. First shadowed angles,

the berried tip of your left breast quick to sip warmth
from the light. My in/drawn breath is both desire
and awe; how this break/able body of yours can hold all

of mine, bucking right back, demanding more, is a miracle
— as is this slow awakening of my flesh, mimicking sunrise.
Waking you is my temptation, but the smile that plays

on your sleeping face is my vanity a/live; I will not kill
it. Instead I muse on the subtle/ties of love; how, to reach
ecstasy, I must be weak for you, let you guide me

as I guide you, no egos fingering the edges of our frailty.
I remember your eyes holding mine, our laughter manic,
nothing between us, knowing how well we fit, how all

our migrations have led to this moment. We spare no energy
for questions, the kind the world's eyes throw at us,
the same way the morning/light separates us into sable/sand.

CONTIGUITY

Separation is a seven-minute walk
taken together, one train stop alone,
followed by another train and an hour's flight
– three hours if you count the formalities
at the airport: the stripping of layers,
a life exposed to x-rays, picking up after.

But it is also walkable miles, days
of silence and three months before

we will be together again. And these metrics,
distance and time, cannot unravel the hours of
your voice's life in my ears, the space the warm
earth essence of you takes up in my nostrils, why
my body in sleep makes space for you
even when my arms can't cradle your flesh.

TRAVELLING SOLO

Coded in smiles and that buzz
we share in the grip of one-
of-a-kind books, paintings, songs…
is a key we both know – one

we build charged chords of joy from,
transpose, dragging 7th notes across days,
twisting distortions into possibility.
We're on a stage and distance is the noise

at the bar; we play harder to rise
above it. The need to make a living
switches tones between major & minor
but we solo our way back to origins;

it's the way we write and don't ♪ it's how
we kiss instantly or hover in hunger – pine ♪
the way, with knowing smiles, we tangle
like some fantasy found in the spine

of a book, two cinnabar shades snug
in the heart of a painting, phrases that
overlap in a song that repeats like a love
supreme, a love supreme ♪ …it's that

way that you hold me ♪ …the way we
hold we ♪ the way you hold hold me
like I'm leaving the melody, knowing
I'm coming back, but still… but still…

BLOWING SMOKE

for the curve of dismounts

o

She lifts her head to gift the stars white
smoke and my lips are drawn to the floral
arch of her neck, inching higher, the swirl
her fragrant exhalations make becoming night:
breath to air, dust to dust — we are mortals
drenched in a hummingbird sensation of time.

oo

I have known moments like this; my naked torso
brown as the bark of the mango tree I've mounted,
its leaves camouflage while I watch my playmates
seeking me, excitement choking me the same way
her moving fingers make my breath hover. She catches
me in the corner of her eye, my lips tremble on her
skin before the giggle becomes sound: lightning to thunder.

ooo

Sometimes I was found — some girl or boy throwing stones,
breaking the amnios of leaves that protected me — but most
times I just got tired of waiting and shimmied down. Love
is a little like that — the playmates plentiful as pollen grains
yet only a few bursting beyond the red bubble of lust
to the heart, the after-giggle, where the smoke rings go.

HOW I KNOW

"I smile a little more than I did before...
That's how I know love." – The RH Factor

Some memory of darkness; soft expanses
of ebony – and flesh that turned liquid
on my tongue, in the clasp of infant gums.
A body that moved to soothe me, a body

with shoulders angled to support leaning.
Notes hidden like silverfish in the creases

of my books, six-year-old fingers turning
care-perfect Ds, surprise declarations that drop
out on stages, reminding me that I've birthed
a girl with heart, a child who knows healing.

The smell of almond and shea butter in the hair
of an embrace, the sound of trains passing, a glut
of air as tunnels fill with weight, slow breath
as I try to hold a moment that feels like one

that shouldn't pass. We're skin to skin at the cheek.
A boy's smile that emerges as his mother's

door closes, his hands reaching for the learned angle
of my shoulders, the circumference of my neck
soon in the clasp of his thighs, monkey-bar antics
fading as a girl warms my cheek with her small hand.

This is how my dad felt, perhaps. All I remember is fleeting,
but I recall the scratch of a pin on shellac, the wound
of Mahalia's voice rising to fill a house, the weight
of his arm around my neck, the whisper of a smile

moving the wood of his skin, his voice saying, *Listen*.
In the poetry section of a bookshop, my hand in the crease

of an anthology of Brazilian poets, lost in the black joy
of word after apt word, I lift my eyes and see the woman
who said yes to dinner. She moves and my mouth is wide;
between us, a field of teeth straining to do more than just smile.

OF SIDES

Love for you is
    what you have
witnessed: doing

something you hate,
proof of sacrifice.
Love weighed in debts:
a chorus of chores.

Love for me is what
    I know: loving
whatever I'm doing

because it is done
for love, done with
song, skip in the heart,
the task forgotten.

Every day you smile
less; my smile becomes
wider. To onlookers it seems
I am consuming you.

I am the one who is
    wronged, but love is
a cushion of many sides.

LOCKING DOORS
(for Teacher & the Sundance Kid)

To free the L from its metal perch, slide
the torpedo of its head into place, locking
the front door. To check the fires of the gas
stove do not still burn... He remembers it's night
and darkness brings duties. He holds your hand,

guides you to the bathroom, turns on the light,
turns away before you turn on him, as you do
sometimes when the cache of your memories reset,
making him a stranger. He can recall Grand National
winners' names for the last twenty-five years: *Don't*

Push It, *Royal Athlete*, *Earth Summit*, *Comply or Die*
... reels them off in his head, while you slip into Igbo,
speaking to the Canadian neighbours who share your South
Eastern patch of London with you, falling back gently,
the way your Romanian gymnastics teacher taught you

in Lagos all those years ago. And this is the beauty
he holds onto: how you can recite his parents' phone number
as though some magic has unlocked the forgotten idyll
of your unsettled Apapa youth. You still remember him
as the boy with a parting trimmed semi-permanently

into his hair by a father he saw when the ships came,
who brought you akara so hot he juggled it all the way
to your house, smiling as he told you he was the one
who got the first ones from the pan, first in the queue. He is
no longer the man who almost gambled your lives away, who

near lost his mind when your twin boys died
at fifteen: no,
he is again the boy
who kissed you and ran towards sunset,
looking back every fifteen metres to see if you were smiling too.

YEAR AD 87: BM14

a poem in three sentences

Before the memory of spit wiped from your brow
in silence, before a boy in blue in Manchester
threatens to put you in *the* van simply for asking

What is our crime? before the grainy 1991 birth
of raised batons caught on camera raining on Rodney,
before Joy Gardner, Roger Sylvester, Erica Garner,

Sandra Bland, Sean Rigg, Cynthia Jarrett turned breathless
under a white haze of hatred, when you only blazed
in protest when you were tackled to the ground playing

football in a swirl of dirt, cheers and jeers raining
from the edges of a rectangle in Accra. / Blue-tinged
days when you were newly teen and only beginning

to edge towards the van of the hormone-driven youth
movement, before you knew the damaging disorientation
of a kiss on the collarbone, a nip beneath the breastbone,

had you been taken to the side one fine Saturday
(after you'd wiped the chequered vinyl floors of your home
on hands and knees, laughed with your siblings

while coaxing the gleam from your parents's cream Volvo
and had your cold water shower while whistling Whitney's
new song, *I Wanna Dance with Somebody*, given lemonade

– pale green and fresh), and told that you would know love
many times over, that your heart would stretch, sing and shatter,
that you would learn the suck and spit of spent bodies,

33

that you would break and bloom, and break and bloom,
but through the mill of that mix of ache and injustice
in the world, you would find yourself a father of three

and friend of a clutch of formidable women you know
so intimately that you could take breaths for them,
you would have jumped up and screamed *No way*!

spilling the lemonade onto dirt like a libation,
your joy too much to contain at such possibility.//
This is how, come Saturday, when you pick your kids

up, you are always so stunned, because who would believe the tooli that
in a world that showers so much terror on skin so dark
you could still make, out of one lemonade-drinking boy so blue,

a full-muscled girl, a wise-cracking boy and a wide-grinning girl?///

A CONCISE GEOGRAPHY OF HEARTBREAK

Human

...it starts from the skin, the same way
   Europeans came from the shore, smiling,
      setting up trading posts. When they whisper
         in your ears, nibble on your lobes, sending
            a shiver running through you, that's Stanley
         pretending to be an explorer, but under contract
   to King Leopold. A finger runs down
  your chest, raising goosebumps, your lips
lock and your oil reserves run free.

Environmental

You are learning
a new language, every limb of your body
possessed by the fire of this love that smelts
gold, aluminium, copper, tin and iron ore. You run

when they ask,
doing do-for-love things, making their lives
easier. Meanwhile, they are with friends planning
how to deceive you, use you – it's the Berlin Conference

in kisses. They are all up inside you,
you are in your feelings, sappy
as sliced rubber trees.

Physical

You want to drop seeds and shit,
hell, maybe you do – one or two –
until some night the forest fires start.

It's like the worst kind of heartburn –
all that BS you've swallowed.
You start an independence movement,

define limits, draw borders. They come pleading,
they offer enticements, ambassadors
make compelling cases, seeding tears

in your eyes. But once you have seen
their true purpose, you can't unsee it: you must
save your heart – even if it means you will hurt,

even if the new country you carve is
an assembly of broken things, it is yours.
You will compose an anthem

and sing it like an orgasm. You will
sew a flag from fragments of new insight,
fly it as high as you hold your head.

UNDERBELLY

You are seven, her eyes are molten,
her chin weighs what your thinking
weighs on the heels of your palms,
your fingers are feathers along the lines
of her cheekbones. She is about to kiss
you, but a gaggle of friends come in
and she spits in your face instead.

You will remember that moment when
you are twenty-eight and you trace
the point when a lover you meant to marry
turned sour on you, to an evening out
with her girlfriends discussing the lure
of unpredictable men. Suddenly she's asking
about circumcision – a new interest in dicks.

The twenty-one year gap in betrayals
hasn't changed you. Your boys don't understand,
neither can the ex's friend who sleeps with you
now: how can you be so calm – happy even?
But your thoughts are feather-light with little
memories: the euphoric pull of dark eyes, loving
moments together, away from the baying crowds.

LENGUAJE

Whisper to me in the language I know
when I know no language, when my face
still bears the map of sleep, the clear trace
of fatigue passing, mute and steady as breath.

Call out at the hour when I am uncertain
whether the sky's clustered darkness threatens
rainfall or signals night fading away.
Coax my protest muscle from my mouth's shell,

coat my lips with a fine dew of argument
and place your morning plea beyond barriers
of translation. Let tongue touch tongue, test,
and by degrees reach fluency in the lingua

that calls forth the earth's children, conjures flesh
from lust. I entreat you with love – in Ga.

KƐ I'TSUI AKA SHWƐ

"You see, I could conceive death,
but I could not conceive betrayal." – Malcolm X

Ojotswalɔ, my heart burns for you like
kpakpo shitɔ spreading jealous green in
the ripeness of my heart —add not salt to
my pain;

kɛ i'sui aka shwɛ. Do not
bury my passions in ŋmlitsa – hard,
formless and scorching in the sun
for I have loved you too much
to merit such disdain.

Kai'mɔ fɔfɔi ni n'kɛ ba o'shia,
smiles we shared over ngai's spat crackle
the songs we sang together, voices
as warm as water in a gbudugbaŋ,

already past language,
violating taboos as we shared kɔmi
kɛ shitɔ with maŋ –
kai mɔ mi nakai'o
kai mɔ mi nakai.

Kɛ i'tsui aka shwɛ. Do not
linger in the wind of our union
like a basket
of didɛ shala;

kaa ha ni e'tɔmi
tamɔ wolɛɛnyo y hunu mli.
Ofainɛ kɛ obaa shi mi'ɛ yaa.
Kɛ i'tsui aka shwɛ;
don't keep leaving and coming back

39

like a gbogbalo, doing a dance I do not
understand, for I love you
too much to learn
to love you again.

DARK SPIRITS

Home half drunk but   with some degree
of faculty left   you find your exes   naked
in bed with the woman you're seeing now   She's her
best journalist self   soft lamplight lapping her
skin's contours as she turns from the lawyer to ask
the anthropologist about shame in cultures that cleave
tight to commensality   The sculptor is studying the clay

of her own nipples   her calves resting on the microbiologist's
thighs   They pay you no mind   not even the blues
singer who said she would die for you   not even
when you strip and perform that ridiculous party trick
with your dick   no hands as you make the little thing
dance left to right   that the novelist adores   You
sulk as the debate shifts to patriarchy   voices

rising as they coax and challenge   leer and laugh
resonant as they agree on your status as a sincere
but flawed feminist   a sympathiser   they say
     The chemistry lecturer spots you   eventually
points   The Kahlo scholar ignites   a fire   right
in the middle of the bed   and their fingers   like
a hundred licking flames beckon you   You feel

the heat of the equator as you lean back   mattress
buckles   the red of the fire pulling your locks
making you scream   Before your fantasies can come
alive   they turn to envelop you   like caterpillars on
sweet fruit   you disappear in the amber of their fusion
     When morning comes   your room is rich   suffused
with the burn and treacly aftertaste of dark dark spirits

EAUX

OSCURA Y SUS OBRAS

i

Three primary colours mixed
in a shallow pot. A blackness
beyond the reach of a scorpion's sting.
I am yet to meet the being
who can unmix paint, restore
the pure pigment the brush's tongue flicked.

ii

For venom's cure comes from venom,
from fangs jibbed like a fountain pen's nib,
is collected in a hollow, injected by hydraulics.
I say I am a dreamer who fills spaces
with wild doodlings; I place diamonds
in the charcoal of sketches, laughter
in bursts of gloom, but God! Who knew
the power that children have
to expand air, to set a ship adrift?

iii

A brush might ask its bearer: which is
darker at night — sea or sky? A body knows
which dark swallows it whole, but will stay
silent. There is a word for that. I go to bed thinking
there is so much space in the world.
Where are the bony legs to kick me, the questions
that punctuate the black like stars? How long
to fill a canvas with textures of night
without hints of blue, streaks of yellow,
the ballast of its memory of sunset's bruise?

iv

One day I'm in a café writing a poem
about arachnids, sketching eight legs
because words are slow to come.
A kid comes over to ask what I'm doing,
his skin dark as my daughter's, his dimple
like my son's. *I'm trying to fill the space*,
I say, looking at my page, the black paint of brooding.

v

If the scene were painted again, the jib
sail rippling gently with air, the vessel silhouetted,
the sun red as a crying eye and sinking,
the water's gleam a smooth carapace… Even
with what it knows now, with the pain to come,
the nights vast as three empty beds, my flesh
would still enter the damp, be swallowed
by its mood until the body, again, moves.

CARESS

i

If I speak often of gardening and day's
slow rise behind the creep of morning sun,
it is because somewhere along my thigh lies
the memory of a tomato plant's jagged leaf
nibbling at my skin at dawn, your hand steady
at my shoulder, your voice gentle in my ear,
pointing out tiny buds that will turn to flower
then fruit. I hold the faded watering can,
its silver sharp against my grip, dark as yours
as we wade between beds of onion and kale,
lettuce both green and red, aubergines that stand
high as my chest – and all the while time unfurls.
Birds bicker in the guava tree behind us, doors
crack open, the light spreads, its lustre caressing
your tight curls as you pull a radish clean out
of the soil, shake it and bite through its red
skin to the crunch of its white flesh, passing
one half to me. We speak nothing, Okomfo,
of origins, but I know you planted all these seeds
and taught me the tender and the harsh, the art
of nurturing them. And this is all I needed
to know of love – ever: a morning before sun,
the beauty of bud, flower and fruit, a father's voice
with birdsong, the tart white secrets in a radish's heart.

* *Okomfo* – a healer or diviner, a role usually inherited

ii

Between his first word and his first love, a boy
goes to Grecian lengths to undermine his mother.
His chores undone, he creeps beyond the horizon
of her view, past milk bush and fallen, rotting petals
from bougainvillea, into the haze of dust raised
by a fury of youths playing football, waits his turn

while idle tongues run loose with tips on how to love
a woman, how to dribble from one foot to the other,
scoop the ball up with a touch light as a feather
and strike – all this before he is first called to play.

He drops a word he retains from his escapades

                    on bare fields
                    by grass-choked open drains
                    in patches of fruit-and-flower-flecked green
                    of the kind cities hide like armpit hair

in the air when his mother calls
and the hand she means to place on his unkempt head,
naturally, bears no tenderness.

                    He scrambles
to shelter by the mongrel that will soon be struck
by lightning, the one whose tongue she despises, waits
for her rage to cool. Thus begins the tutelage
of a man, salvaged from masculinity.

And now he remembers the strength of her shoulders;
her firm ripostes when, because of her short-cropped hair,
men dared call her *small girl,* whistle across the road;
caress of her hand on his neck as she reproved
a teacher for caning him for his forthrightness;
her anklet of coloured glass beads that never broke.

iii

It is easy to be misled when your head lies
in the lap of a lover who promises all
the things you want your life to be filled with, without
so much as a skipped heartbeat. You will learn later
that a cricket's vow is not the same as an elephant's, that soft
caresses at the pressure point where the ear's flesh
meets the skin behind your high cheekbones can shapeshift
into something deadly on a whim, but for now –
how sweet it is to be loved – you believe it all.
You will live in the sun like your grandfather did,
your children will know the thud of avocados
and mangoes falling unbidden from trees at dawn;
they will speak with your tongue, they will know both your songs.

It is easy to forget in those treacle-sweet
moments the inflection in your name that signals
you have ancestors still owed for their hard labour
in the split rock and damp of the Americas,
how you can't be beholden to the mediocre
since your very intestines are echo chambers
of dreams swallowed under an umbrella of whips.

In the cavern of a kiss, how easily things slide
to the back of the mind – gone, your father's lessons
on how to fondle fruit, to tease the tender skin
with fingers to fathom the ephemeral line
between ripe and rotten, so you are lost, tumbling
in a vortex of broken promises, guilt trips
and misused savings. This is what becomes of your heart
just before it breaks and you begin to claw back
yourself:

your blood is hybrid; your tongue is mongrel,
you carry songs of refuge – refugee mysteries

in the loom of Maroon shanties that shift language.
Your father has been taken, his own father gone,
father upon father, across borders' echo,

and the sea waves back; your skin is weatherbeaten
and it absorbs sun, hatred, fire and shea butter –
it doesn't crack. Summertime and you're still living.
Pick up your pieces by the only light that still
glows – the fading flower of your mother's smile.

iv

My daughter dives, clean as a lemongrass blade
cut into water and something in her, some sheen
of worry is extinguished as her long arms brush
what was still into acceleration. She comes
alive, her head bobbing in and out between breaths.
My mother's shoulders unfurl in her butterfly
strokes, my father's limbs contract every time she turns.
She is calm – luminous in a way I am not
when I swim; I find my release in word and song

instead, knowing sometimes the precise tune I crave
and what souvenirs it carries. Entire affairs
live with me in this way, in gaps between horn solos,
the catch in Ella's voice before Satchmo's
refrain
                    . :
One day my daughter will remember,
as I did when she was born, a long-buried song
that emerges in snippets, swaddled in memory
                                        if you ask me
I could write a book...
                                nkɛ bo baa ya
nkɛ bo baa ya da daa...
                                    then a melody too
she has forgotten the words for, but flowers still
beneath her lips.

            A baby cries, its mouth
a dark, dried fruit, and from somewhere
your entire inheritance of comfort comes
tumbling forth: heartbeat, caress, the first
words that stilled the waters
            when you entered the world:
                                kaa fo.

v

Sometimes a man wakes with Spanish phrases
in his head, with no clear reason beyond a few
hours spent in Madrid, Lima and Buenos Aires.
There is no hand on his chest, no man or woman
calling from another room to ask what he will have
with his coffee, no skin-borne memory of caresses
        just
mala hierba, which is a snippet of something
overheard and *hablemos de la sensualidad*
which he can only imagine is the fruit of a history
of building languages from scraps gathered
in the crowds and markets of Accra, Kumasi,
Cape Coast and Manila: Twi, Ewe, Tagalog, Fantsi.
There might be yet more in the bud
of his heritage: with a great-gran from Fernando Po
and others retrieved to the mother continent
from Guadeloupe, Nova Scotia, Jamaica...
Who can ever tell what words he will scream
should he wake and find his head
replaced with flowers, his eyes stamens,
his cheeks a mesh of petals, pollen scattering
        every time he speaks.

vi

You learn a thing from one lover, use it on another
and he can tell, like she can tell, some frisson
has shifted, some odd flavour lingers

in the fruit of your release.
The question will be asked

later, when seasons have passed and sunflowers gone
to seed, why you lied about it, why you tried
to juggle with the face of a clown,
to creep with an elephant's step.

Was there no father to whisper to you
at dawn which seed belonged to which plant,
which plant to which seed? No mother
to tutor your mouth to speak its desires
kindly, to tell you your heart does not belong
to the hand that caresses your breast?

By then, no answer will return
the body's unquestioning surrender
or the harvests of swaying sorghum,
yam (its mounds so difficult to master),

cocoa and the wild hibiscus so trendy now
in West African bars. But know this:

you will always be loved. You will find
your heart does not need the flint
of broken promises to blossom into flame.

vii

One child I planted tomatoes with,
because for a time there was a patch
of gardening space and sun; another

spoke beautifully with my tongue,
his eyes set in his grandfather's face;
a third held me by the mouth,

kissed me, caressed my cheek
and said *Daddy*, making my heart
thud at dawn each time I remember.

There are songs I have sung to all
my children, words I stole from tunes
shaped in the mouth of my mother.

Thus the body is echo chamber
and memory; all its parts triggers,
every bruise history, melody.

I carry all my dreams; not as I imagined,
but the heft holds – every flower has
fallen to yield some peculiar fruit.

viii

Absence is silence he has learned
to endure, but sometimes it breaks
his faith in his own existence, makes him
rephrase questions: *If a tree falls in a forest
and you don't hear it, do you exist?* Maybe
this is why he hums against the wood
of his own headboard, why it is no surprise

     that *Amazing Grace* is the song
        an agnostic chooses
           to learn
           to play
           on his
           new
         trumpet.

Because it has a history that will see him
past the clumsy blasts of air
he tries to tame into something
more than a noise, something
recognisable, something
he has heard his mother sing before,
with notes his father played – words alive
in the hymn book that survived
his grandmother; a chain that holds them
all, a link that keeps everyone present
in his struggle – free as wind, breath.

One day his children will laugh at him
when he stumbles demonstrating a somersault
and falls with the thud of soft fruit in the morning.
He will chase them in mock fury and try again
and soon he will find ways of teaching them
things he can no longer do himself, like seed

begat bud and bud, flower — a chain unbroken.
Even talents that have slept within him like French
double Ls, alleles in the helix of his life,
he will pass on, easy as the caress that stripped
their mother's body, simple as a song
that beyond silence

lives on.

ix

If I speak now of day's orange retreat and the lily
white of a moon's rise, it is because
one dusk a kayak will lick the face
of Lake Volta, slick as a boat that once glided,
a man in its belly, towards the flower
of Guadeloupe. In it will be
a woman,
breath warm in light breeze,
her dark shadow skimming ripples –
island bound. You will neither see the fruit
in her lap, nor the seed in the fruit.
You will not hear the song
in her head. It is said
no man is an island, but perhaps
a woman is
because an island will bud,
will flower, will fruit – an island
knows the history-filled caress
of a bone-heavy sea, wet and clean
as glass; an island can hide rebels in its green,
can feed them bread as fruit and red flowers
as liquid; an island
can birth a man.

YORKSHIRE BATH DISPLAYS
(or *six ways of looking at a bath with dark brown legs walking the streets in northern England*)

i – theft

The damn thing is stolen, he is
carrying it over his head
to evade cameras: cheeky lot,
these darkies, he's using the overflow
hole for eyes.

ii – migration

See what people will do to avoid paying
for a taxi? That would be what? Fifteen
quid? These immigrants are just tight-
            fisted. It's ridiculous. ridiculous!

iii – africans

Africans! They can't stop carrying things
on their heads if they try. Imagine
            that! Lugging a bath across Leeds
on your head – remember that Yeboah fella?
He could strike a ball like a sledgehammer.

iv – theatre

It's got to be one of those

new performance thingies. To see

people's reactions, like. Didn't you *hear*
about the one they did in a beetle? I am
surprised that little thing

didn't fall apart

v – truth

NIGHT: A Yorkshireman steals
a moment away from the bed, where
his children sleep, to rediscover his wife
in the bath. Her immigrant hands clenched

tight, he adjusts his head to carry
the weight of her pleasure on his tongue.
The contortions of their play, the heft
of his Caribbean roots and the ink of her

Indian know/ledge, wobble the tub's legs.
It falls to the ground, water sloshing
like the Aire on a windy day. Surprisingly
the children do not stir, do not wake.

vi – summary

DAY: Buying a new bath is easy, getting
a van on a bank holiday is tricky – and…
hailing a taxi while west/black has many stories;
hailing a taxi while carrying a white bath is
                                        another.

THE FURNACE

When you spend your childhood bathing
with cold water, you learn – quick
as lime – that soap

is warm enough to hold
back the chill of night
caught in bound oxygen;

that although moving fast will help,
it's better to stay even,
let your body heat find equilibrium;

that the earth takes the full brunt
of the sun's burning
so it can guerrilla through the veins

of the water system
to infuse your post-football shower
with unexpected joy;

that your father carries the fires
of all his disappointments
under the coal of his skin; that

your mother's embrace is a furnace.

INHERITANCE

Sometimes I overhear the muted
susurrations of worms bent as hooks
into leaf-rich mounds of soil, the plea
of voices not meant for my ears. It is

gossip, calculated as a rocket's purest
arc, promises slipped into the ears of lovers,
hackneyed phrases like *you're only as young as*
you feel – and my mind drifts to you; how

all your life you cried like a baby – never
controlled – your face a network of creases
that mapped your pain. You were my father
and I learned to love you with your face wet.

This may be
a twisted way
of saying thanks

for teaching me that even a life of nights still
whispers the sun's burn, that the fluid of one's
tears do not make the body boneless; it takes
strength to show how you feel but not waver

in your resolve, knowing the hourglass of healing
never loses its sand. As a boy, seeing you cry freed me,
pulled me from the vortex enough times to outspin
an unremarkable life. I have walked from light

into the comforts of darkness – rebirth canals –
confident that a path will unfold, the way
I did after I held dark soil in my teenage hands
and cast it on the wood of your departure, the way

this poem begins
with the invisible
prompting of ghosts

and ends with the soft lines of a questing pen,
like the earth cycling with the turning of nematodes
silent as DNA
                    in the darkness beneath my feet.

11-PAGE LETTER TO (A)NYEMI (A)KPA

for Kakaiku & Ma Rainey

i - *signs*

Blood of mine, it is said… it was… an uncle
said someone has to stay behind, to receive
the letters, to tell the story (though not at leave
to read), but we both know that's a Brer ruse,
a cousin-saving con. You stayed to flatten yourself
into signposts pointing away from where we fled to.
Brown as tree bark, expression wooden, you burned;
loath to give me up, you flamed as my wings bent.
I became wind; you became smoke – I see your signature
before it rains. I pour libation for your sacrifice;
your children sprinkle from 40s for my disappearance.

ii - *lizards*

It was as old Tom Wilson said later, Anyemi,
safer among the alligators, the swamp's embrace
making mist of my tracks, shapeshifting my glaze
into scales. It was a measure of my fever that I fled,
one white man to fight alongside another, held loyal
for a cold, hard promise. It's the price of the ticket,
the cost of return: a will folded as achingly as our bodies
when we were tallied and shipped here. When you're ready,
Omanfo, when we sit one day to the agreement of two lizards –
one orange-flecked, the other with an orange band, you'll see:
I'll tell you how my veins knew ice to a Nova Scotian degree.

iii - *passing*

One freezing night, in a dream, a pair of antlers
threw shadows hard as jail bars, cut across a wasteland,
blurred my vision. When I awoke I was unsure if the twin
shapes stood for us, but there is a proverb I now know,
Manyo: two antelopes do not solely roam for companionship
– one eats, the other watches. You didn't flinch at the crossroad,
i'naa nabi, your genius for metaphor already clear as mead –
you factorised the 3/5 skewed algebra of liberation down
to (me -white) (you +white); you chose the plus sign,
you would ghost-pass: if phantoms are white, death is free.
Your cousin got freedom. I haven't stopped moving since.

iv - *earth, wind, water*

Your totems hum still in the shrines we nested
in trees, before ill winds blew white sheets to anchor
cargoes of wood and breathing greed off our warm shores.
Did we guess, or did we know — to riddle our prayers
into the pores of the earth herself, the rivers ciphered
slick with warnings? They began with mirrors, changeable
as their skins under sun, before they looted masks
with empty eyes — hollow songs, stretched goatskin under
untutored hands. Dead goats on their own cannot bleat
the drum's message; all the earth's miles can't sever song
from your tongue. I see your off/spring dance our river'(s)kin

v - fire

I will not speak of fire. You did not burn. Let me
tell you what I've learned: in one language, fire is
also invitation; you change the tone in another – blood;
in a third, fire is your father. It is not prestidigitation
that smoke casts shadows. You are the invisible man, Anyemi,
the woman at the back of a bus; I am the one who reclaimed
my name. I am my father's second son – if I am missing
the first will be questioned. This is how our absence was
marked: girls and boys eating with twin names, no one to watch,
fingers squeezing otɔ, but too distracted to know its fire –
an antelope with a single antler carries pain in the neck.

vi - *bones*

Achingly, a folded wing, I'm a boomerang in black soil.
Before I returned to the hem of our rivers I believed
we had been forgotten. But how could we be?
We are words fallen from a language, coral on the tongue,
stuck in a line of fiber-optic bones marrowing the Atlantic,
pentatonic notes our key clue – listen to the melody:
the heart is an aviary, its treasure of birds not always visible,
but look at these bright feathers we flag into gay fabric!
Lorde-led now, we unschool lies woven into our daily
routine to learn again the languages that will teach us
to dance the dance of twins, the dance of abusua as army.

vii — *paper*

Some mornings my eyes water with your wounds, all
the tiny hairs that must have taunted the flames
before they spread their tongues on your skin. I am free
because you are smoke. I think of memory as retained folds
in paper that was once origami; I think of memory
as the layers an onion holds; both of them fade
in heat but something lingers; this be the twist
of DNA that syllabled Ebonics. Any rapper will know this;
that language is paper, that onions turn translucent
but collards stay green. I'm applauding you from outchea
money — mo, mo, mo, mo, mo, mo, mo, mo, mo, mo, mo.

viii – *language*

When we pour schnapps on the earth, when you tip
liquor onto concrete, it does not trickle into graves.
There is a place called sɛɛsane where the trees bloom
with hindsight; this is where our dear departed sit –
ancestors side-by-side with boys assassinated for skin
crimes: this is Africa, this is America. Our nyɛmɛɛ
and sisters have been showing them the charts, unspooling
the con: in that world darkness defines kinship
not language. Remember the snippets of that Song
of Solomon: *because I am black; our bed is green… through
the lattice.* Language is lattice – we are whole behind it.

ix — *cracks/stone*

I have learned the caution of geckos. Black
and pale, they pale into the cracks of barriers;
when they lose a tail it grows back. We have a history
hacked off by marauders; what we're taught now is knowledge
without a body. My grandmother on home soil was one
of the first trained midwives, we are told. We are left,
though, with the mystery of her miracle birth; who first
cut the cord that bound her to water? Who delivered
all those babies on the plantations in the wading years before
their bodies were allowed to cross the threshold of hospitals
their chattelled fathers muscled out of rocks both black and pale?

If we have so many words for family, how
can you be gone? Brer, Anyemi, Omanfo – how
were we broken? I am thinking now of subtraction;
perhaps that is the unspoken angle, the unused eye?
The one whose fortune it is to stay behind may be as blessed
as cursed, for what becomes of the remainder after
the division? That little (r) stuck to its side like a sca(r)
while the rest take the ska? Breaking that beat, Money,
nobody is taken without family left behind, no chariot
rolls without leaving tracks. There are tears in our wake
enough to raise Jordan. The sea between us is common salt.

xi — *helix*

Listen, Ma, if between rainy days and blue skies
some fool asks you to prove it, don't bother with ancestry
websites; I know by the way you walk you took fire
for me; I can hear in your voice the drums they forbade
you to play. Our unspoken pact was to somehow survive.
So hold my hands now, Ace, and let's reshuffle, throw
out the balm of forgetting, read the boomerang's marked hide.
You are no longer an antelope alone — we are an entire
herd. You can wade in the water. I'm looking out for you.
My antlers, like yours, (r) an eleven (11) on the head: multiplied
we equal 121 — one-to-one let's unravel helices, let's talk.

* *Brer, Anyemi, Omanfo, Manyo, I'naa nabi, Money, Ma, Ace, Abusua —*
various words/slang for addressing family members

TREE OF THE INVISIBLE MAN

I can say nothing of its name, save the name
of the factory behind which it stood, the one bleeding
dyes all day, making gutters that once were streams
a carnival of bright death – green, red: Golden

Textiles. The tree itself was a lesson in the art
of contortion, its hard angles an eloquent semaphore,
clear lines of survival under abuse. It had a hole
right through its trunk. First we peeked through it,

but months later we stopped, only to see who could
        make a matching chink
            through cellulose
    – that narrow
     body. I see its shape now as I close my eyes, the seven
punctures we managed to riddle it with, the pens it cost us,

coat hangers, twisted forks, a stolen corkscrew, the pale
gleam of those offerings at its base when the sun set;
the view through the gaps if you stepped back – squinted,
as though the eight holes were one, no bark between.

Its dark roughness is the skin I inhabit in this dream
where I'm away from home, visible as a threat, unnoticed
though breathing. I count the bullets shot by ganged boys
in blue, measure their circumference against my skin:

calibre, quantity per dark double, drawing a map of round
          fissures where my flesh should be,
     flood of projectiles at my feet. The view
           clears as I squint,
my reflection shines

like water at sunset.
The whole widens.

One night, I am all mirror — no flesh.

DEFENCES

i

You must learn to walk on water, if you want
to live in a place that does not flood.
You raise your eyebrows levée-like and I nod

thinking of how beneath the highs of cities
like Paris and New York, beyond the accessible depths
of Metro and Subway, the mapped grids where

you can pay to travel to hearth or heartbreak,
there are conduits for liquid: tunnels, storm
drains large enough to harbour a parade of liars.

ii

When my uncle Freddie dies
you hold my hand in a damp grip,
which reminds me of our first sweat-
heavy coupling in Accra under a fan,

while I tell you stories my father told
me about Freddie's incredible prowess
at sport, how he later escaped
a kidnap plot by a corrupt government
by hiding in the boot of a Welsh
lecturer's car as she drove to Abidjan

for a weekend tryst. But we are
both stunned at his funeral as three
previously unknown children of his
emerge from beneath the high pitch
of the voice reading his obituary,
their eyes damp with love that belies

distance. They will later reveal
that one weekend a month he collected
each of them from their mothers,
took them to a quiet beach house

with a view of the stars. He fed them
breakfasts of fresh fish, grilled
on the shore, taught them sprinting
and salsa, talked about physics

and politics. Strange but wonderful
father, they say, after you have
wiped my tears with your pinky.

iii

One day, when we are no longer together
I find myself under a fan in Singapore

thinking about the sheen of sweat that brewed
on your skin when we made love, the glow

fired from the blood vessels beneath it –
all ten thousand kilometres of them alive

to the transition we were making from steady
to ecstatic; how you tried to hold in your screams

and dissolved into manic giggles – your thighs clamps,
my body iron. I reflect on those moments anew

because the woman resting on my bare back
in the humid Straits afternoon has sweat
far less salty than yours and it set me

thinking about storm drains and what secrets
lie in the water they carry, the seas they empty
into, how you can never tell how much

salt hides in a tear
                    or a drop of sweat
without letting it ride
the ridges of your tongue.

And if the heart pumps blood
and blood is ninety-two percent water,
how much salt

will sour a heart?
Whose water gets walked on?

SUB.MARINE.BLUES

sub

This one
is like midnight sea,
dark and powerful,
lashed

with ripples over an age-
old soul.
There are grey foam patches
in the night
of his head.

That one
is like midnight seen
predictably dense,
hunched

over his own seed,
unaware of time,
determined still to change
everything ductile
to string ends.

And this one goes still to sea,
though less now.

He has taken what he can
and mainly mends nets

in blue arcs
contoured by experience
to eke the best years
out of a fishing net.

Yet that one rips them
far too frequently;
dragging smiles
from this one who knows
failure is heard

louder than advice.
That
one will learn,
and who knows

if midnight is the child
of midnight sea
since neither is permanent
though one is more
tangible.

But these men pull both in
from seventeen to seventy;

hand following hand
father after son

and never have their boats lacked
a man
to go
to sea.

marine

The story is told of one
old fisherman who woke up
in the dead of night, yelled
ee'ba eei, ee'ba kɛ loo

("It is coming
it is laden with fish.")
So deep
did the rhythm of the tides throb
in his veins, that he sensed

the moment
the jubilant buoys
began
to drift back to shore.

Sure,
these men don't see
in the submarine darkness
of their calling, they feel.
Isolated from the stability of land,

they use stars for landmarks
and seek their dreams in the reflections

of heaven. In the old man's youth
they would push their canoes out

until half submerged
in blue, then they paddled smooth
as beaten leather, leaving
lather in their wake

and messages sketched

on the sea's veneer
by their trailing nets.
Nnw, the guttural grunts of gunmetal
black outboard motors

violate air and sea
as they Doppler
in and out of view
at double the speed,

the canoes stabbing
urgently against the horizon.
The old men sit
at the water's end
barefoot

on the battered shells of worn-out vessels
sharing tales of those who did not return,

weaving webs of blue into broken nets.
Occasionally they help pull in the laden nets.

"Ee'ba eei," they yell; "it is coming",
watching the nearing boats, the buoys marking
the net edges, taking care not to wade out
too far.

blues

Greek mythological claims
of the greatest beauties
and most powerful gods
stem from saved documents,

but truth cannot be written.
The many nets of interpretation
it filters through before it pen-drops
onto sheet extracts
its solid claims,

like fish from a hyperbolic sea.
These men's catch is passed on
to their wives for sale
and most are happy with this

arrangement.
So the wives dot the shoreline
with grin-like glints angling off
their hand-beaten aluminium pans
as their voices soar
over the collusion of waves

to sing out the price of fish.
The women wrap patterned cloth around

their breasts, the knots of which serve
as carriers for their earnings.

At night, these women slide
money like dreams
into the men's hands
to buy comfort

in alcoholic volumes —
and volumes of these sea-blue-
blooded men have passed unseen
to the other side.
It is said

that water maidens
in glowing raiment listen in
on their drunken speech
and cast blue spells

upon the disgruntled.
With woven diamond fingers
and meshes of cotton onyx hair
they hypnotise, their cowrie
beaded hips sinuous as waves.

Their complexion is whatever the water gives,
their touch is the toe caress of dying waves;

their smile is sunset on an overturned horizon
and their kiss is a blend of amnesia and ambrosia.

These are the world's greatest
beauties!
They leave men dumb-founded,
floundering in invisible waves.

The disgruntled never re-emerge,
they vanish after consecutive evenings seen
staring out over the sea — copper blue
like sub marine greek
statues.

ZEST

OUR LOVE IS HERE TO STAY

Clouds gather under a blue moon,
like trouble brewing as strange fruit
continues to swing – keeping time –
while Columbia turntables refuse to spin
the song. Is vinyl too black, too flash to be
sleeved in white prisons? The answer lies

like white gardenia petals on a bruise
too subtle to separate from wind; like
a trumpet caught in the ill wind of a jet's
prejudice in the company of clouds – a
rumble in a jungle of noise, the forgotten b-
side that holds its breath. Trouble brewing.

There's nothing random about rain;
It clears the sky's throat for the sun's shrill
voice; the white hanky is for black sweat.

They'll all laugh when I say it, whisper
as though I'm making whoopee with Communist
ideals. They'll laugh like they laughed
when Louis appeared coal-sketched on screen,
years before he lifted the smoke and called
Eisenhower a spade, said let's call the whole

Soviet thing off, as sweetly as he sang *that song*
with Ella ___ and there's silence where the applause
should be; because it's OK when the needle hits
the dark flesh of wax and causes blue screams,
but when the tip hits the dark flesh of a woman
and she wails for justice, shooting off ideas

as she reloads stimulants, suddenly music is
treble trouble. And everybody knows
that the calm comes before the clouds...

There's nothing random about rain, so blow
Louis, blow from cheek to cheek, blow
under a blanket of blue until you get a kick
from a laughing Ella and switch the tone
so swift   //   so hot   //   so dark
that the only bright thing will be the spotlight

of struggle illuminating a girl in Baltimore,
learning as time goes by that life isn't a fine
romance, love, but your soul won't desert you;
like the note can't leave the music, like
the shadows can't leave the darkness.
The secret is to listen; to the slow creeping

embrace of the trumpet's protest, the percussive
defiance of the piano's syncopation, the indrawn
breaths when the song learns the body that sings it.

CROSSROAD VS BLUES
(or *You Wouldn't Talk About Crossroads If You Knew My Life*)

> "*I went to the crossroad, fell down on my knees*
> *...standin' at the crossroad, tried to flag a ride...*
> *didn't nobody seem to know me, babe, everybody pass me by*"
> — Robert Johnson

Belly

I see a road growing branches, but these hands sure can swing an axe
I see a jungle of confusion, but these hands still can swing an axe
Come hell or highest water, I'll still be on the road making tracks

I came up on Fannin' Street, with just a guitar and walking shoes
All the halls and saloons in Bottom, with a guitar and walking shoes
(I) met 'leggers, girls and hustlers, came away singing Shreveport blues

Got mighty fine stories, stranger; I don't need to make no deals
Got a chain of chanting work songs; I don't need to make no deals
Hand me my 12-string over yonder; I'll show how the blues are
       meant to feel

It's Huddie, Sal's little boy, but e'erybody calls me Lead Belly
I'm promised to sweet Martha, but on the road I'm Lead Belly
Even jailers couldn't hold me, once I made them hear me clearly.

Buddy

I picked balls before strings, so my tunes all carry weight
I started with diddly, arms strong from lifting cotton bales
Two-fifty to the two-string, all my stories carry weight

I crossed roads with my tow truck, but I never hung around
Baton Rouge to Chicago, Friendly Chap never hung around
If you needed to find me, I was where the folks was brown

I cook a mean rack of ribs; I learned that from my mama
(I) play a polka dot Strat; I do that for my mama
and I don't need to do no deals, don't need that type of drama

I learned the licks by listening, then plucking by ear
I've been playing these blues ten dozen nights a year
When streets are bare and night has fallen, I'll still be playing here.

Rosetta

I was told I'd see some creature; all I see is a raft
I was warned to take a preacher; all I see's a bobbing raft
I don't need no floating lyrics cos I was born with the craft

Had my own words since I was four; in church I made my voice strong
Had an axe since I was four; it's how this girl got her freedom
I don't need no outside hand, cos I build my own kingdom

Who needs a night devil when a girl's got black magic?
Who needs a night devil when a girl's got black magic?
Don't it take you close to heaven when you hear my guitar lick?

I take light into the dark, I see strange things everyday
(I) take my Gibson into basements, I see strange things everyday
I rock harder than high rollers, but the blues showed me the way.

Stevie

Had a mean old daddy, his hands rained pretty heavy
Had a sour-faced old man whose palms were rough and heavy
I learned real, real quick, Stevie gotta take care of Stevie

As a boy I turned to Mama, but she was weak for his kisses
See, Mama had a strong arm, but she was weak for his kisses
A sharecropper's girl, she sure knew what the blues is

Cos Mama wouldn't leave him, we were caught at his crossroad
(Me) and my brother Jimmy, used guitars to find our slip road
Till spinning crossroads come for me, I'll be on the road

When it comes down to choosing, I'm my mama's boy
Don't waste my time with the devil, I am my mama's boy
She couldn't leave Daddy's slow hand; I use my hands for joy.

Howling Wolf

Howling, howling, but I never saw no wolf
Red Rooster rustler, I've been howling since my youth
But when I found the blues in Patton, I knew I'd found the truth

What's all this racket? All this talk of Devil deals?
I stand six-foot-three, look like the Devil's nemesis
My mama's rejection showed me what my path was

I played Lemon, I played Rainey, played every hour I could
Sonny Boy taught me harp, Charley's licks made my guitar smooth
(I) got dragged into the army, but still made my way to school

Drove up to Chicago, with pockets full of dough
Paid everyone I played with, never cheated a soul
If I'm not in the spotlight, ask Lillie if I made it home.

Robert Johnson

Know that song of 27? First riff on that comes from me
and I'm an endless rambler, jump on every train I see
but ain't never met no devil, unless they came to see me

(I) played in many hellholes, still couldn't pay my bills
Till 100 past my birthday, gals were my only other thrill
If you take away my music, there's nothing more to reveal

In my head I hear boogie and turn it blue on my strings
Just like Zimmerman taught me, I pluck these blues from my strings
Watch me sing my heart out on corners, like an angel floats on wings

Call me invisible, call me ghost – you won't forget my name
Number 11 of my mama's children, you won't forget my name
Hear blues, rock and roll playing and know I changed the game.

Ma Rainey

Can't nobody hold me back, baby, Ma Rainey is my name
I always made my own damn way, Ma Rainey is my name
I wear a collar, tie and gold teeth when I come out to play

First hit me in Missouri, been singing the blues ever since
Gripped me like a lover's thighs, I've been hooked ever since
Went on the road like See See Rider, my smile gleaming like flint

Did I come in April or September, Georgia or Alabama?
See I'm hard to pin down, I'm slippery as a spinning spectre
Why go to the crossroads when the world spins around my centre?

I'm the first, I'm the mama, I'm nobody's coon shouter
Call me names, I'll knock you down, you can't prove it on me after
I worked hard, paid my dues, my songs will ring in the hereafter.

Slim Gaillard

Slim slam flim flam vouto is my McVouty voodoo
If you know the blues, ain't no need to translate for you
You can jive and have a ball, it still reaches into you

Every pack has a wildcard and I ran wild all my life
If you ask me what the blues is, I'll open the book of my life
Stranded in Greece as a boy, but, man, I turned out fine

My guitar weeps blues, my voice scats in jazz
If music were a crossroad, I'd be the question to ask
There's no deal to hold down a language that moves so fast

The twelve-bar is everybody's bar; we all drink out there
Jelly Roll, Louis and Duke, they all hang out there
I scat around the crossroad, cos there's no devil to fear.

Muddy Waters

My grandmama called me Muddy, the Waters came with the harp
You might think you know my blues, but you don't know the half
(A) sharecropper's measly wages is how I bought my first guitar

Had my own joint by eighteen, listened to the blues all day through
Like the waters of the Mississippi, the flow of it stays inside you
Anyone from the hell of plantations, loves water and feels the blues

A boy raised in hell don't make deals with the devil on the side
(I) heard my own voice played on the juke and knew I had heaven inside
Stayed with my grandmama a little longer, but I knew I had heaven inside

Only deals I ever make are with good ole Willie Dixon
He gives me all the right words when my blues need fixing
My archive runs deep as water, all rolling stones need my benediction.

Big Mama Thornton

A church singer's daughter from Alabama, I'm the original Big Mama
Bessie Smith and Memphis Minnie, their voices were my teachers
I can sing high, I can sing low, cos my daddy was a preacher

I was on stage before Elvis, he ain't nothing but my hind dog, I say
And when Janis Joplin copied Ball & Chain, Bay-Tree took all the money
When you've met real-life devils, who needs to go to the crossroads to play?

I can beat my own drum and I play the harp pretty good
I made music with all the good guys, with Muddy and BB too
And everybody knows I don't need no microphone to sing my blues

You'll find me where there's *good singing* and the liquor supply's ample
I may not be wearing no dress, but you'll know me by my dimple
Feet on the ground, singing from my heart; I'm one of the blues's finest examples.

Blind Lemon Jefferson

East Texas streets is where I fine-tuned my blues
In bootleg corners with bad men and fine women, a blind man singing blues
Couldn't work with the sharecroppers so this is how I put my hands to use

Been at a hundred crossroads, but I ain't heard nothing but revelling
Stories about devils is how they pretend we didn't rise by struggling
I'll record 100 songs in thirty-six months and every one will be sterling

See I'm so damn original, even the devil couldn't copy me
With my quick-fingered magic, there ain't many that can play like me
When B.B. King holds Lucille sometimes he tries to sound like me

They call me Blind Lemon Jefferson, sweet and high is how I sing
When T-Bone was starting out, he walked with me and I guided him
My sound is so indescribable, I leave black snakes moaning.

Big Bill Broonzy

Odd jobs by day, guitar by night; that's how I made it
One of seventeen kids, I know how to work till I make it
From the fiddle to the guitar, I pulled strings till I nailed it

Played the two-stages but went to war for everyone as one
Now I write my own tunes; don't need no crossroads plan
Got rights to more than 300 songs and the devil ain't got none

(I) got the keys to the highway so I ain't afraid of the road
Opening for folks who don't know struggle, but I ain't afraid of the road
I've got a boy out down under; I made him on the road

Got the blues from childhood and I've played it near thirty years
I cooked, swept and carried loads. but the blues still rang in my ears
So I picked up this guitar and you'll be hearing me for years.

INTERPRETATION

You can't have heard
the one about the butcher who became
a classical conductor. It is
said he coaxed blood from warm flesh
the same way he makes strings whine
and horns mimic a bull's lament in allegro.

His feeling for time signatures as true
and unshifting as an Accra sunset,
you can set a seed's germination into pale
clef-shaped shoot by his baton,
his restless foot, the shapes his body forms
as he conjures sound and silence.

Audiences flock to see him lead
virtuosos from the highest high to the deep;
he gives new life to the Mendelssohn woman –
Fanny – buries old notions of Beethoven and Rachmaninov,
but, as with all music, interpretation varies
and the historic question hovers always in the air

like a trenchant treble in an echo chamber
of wonder. Was he a butcher of livestock
or of men? Was his past work in an abattoir
or a boardroom? Did any of his victims
lean their heads into the curve of a melody,
sun striking one ear, tuned for the song's end?

#LABOUR

Two girls are tending a sick calf, kneeling
in the direction of Mecca. I would call it

worship, except religions have spoiled the heart
of these simple acts: of a body moving and finding

orientation; of hands placed on flesh to help
with healing. A haze of dust hangs in the air;

the criss-cross sticks of a Moringa fence makes a grid
that frames their labour. The calf is twisting, but still

on the floor. There is no sign of its mother. One girl
strokes its back. Her scarf is made from a piece

of Presbyterian Church anniversary cloth. The other
girl wears knock-off Off-White trainers, conceived

by a designer favoured by Rihanna and Louis Vuitton,
an Ablorh with family roots enshrined less than 400km

away from the earth she crouches on. With coaxing, the calf
finds its feet. Unsteady at first, it regains balance and turns

to lick the hand of the Presbyterian girl. Both girls
dust off their long, bright skirts, rising as the sun sets.

MOONWALK

Once you nail it, you're hooked as a baby
that's discovered rhythm; round a bright corner
and back; in the middle of a mate's party
the crowd parting as if you have dark wands
for legs — skill becoming reflex. It won't hit you
until after your fifth heartbreak, the probability
that your lust to go back to the lover before
the last, might be linked to that rapid flick

of Michael Joseph's glove before he floats backwards.
After all, whatever problems you might have had
with the old flames, there's been reflection. Funny how
you forget the petty flash points of your rows,
but can recall exactly how they made your skin tingle,
the imprint of their lips at the tips of your fingers

still a phantom that can resurrect shivers.
What's important is that, for now, it's just an urge;
you know cause and effect is never simple; you know
MJJ learned that move from someone; you've heard
his father beat him; you know your own daddy
used to slap your mummy. She'd lift you by
your arms, leave… but always returned. The music
his pleading made was an addiction she couldn't shake

till he died. And that whole vial of time, you hid
in your room, rewinding that Maxell, stopping the tape
at the point in "Billie Jean" when that bass rhythm hits,
then pressing play, the song's protest surging forth
while you learned to glide, back, back, back, pause,
shimmy, the volume rising over arguments, your heels

repelling each other like magnets, never touching earth.

TO BE IN LOVE

Sometimes love is static, that ancient
honed vinyl crackle, tagging along easy,
a groupie bearing the bounty of beats,
B-flat horns, Hammond highs and double
bass staccatos that make a classic song.
If your father ever missed a record's release
it was due to some lure your mother conjured;
if he didn't, the record's pull surpassed the gleam
of the lips Mother smiled with. It was love

either way. Imagine how, out of a lifetime
hoard, he wakes one weekend to curate for you
a selection of songs, letting the 33⅓s spin
as he records them onto magnetic tapes he will
pass on. Stickler for detail, he adjusts volume
levels so Lateef's horn will not suddenly drown
Masekela's "Lady" when the songs lean to transition.
He will die soon after you have learned to love
the five tapes he labelled for you; technology

will move on and you will stop playing them,
listening to "A Little 3/4 for God & Co" as MP3
instead of on the old grey machine that clicks
with a familiar cushioned resistance in the dark
before the motor starts its coordinated roll,
before the sound lifts the hem of the invisible.
But some blue day, your heart broken, sorting
through the detritus of an eternal love
that just failed to make a full fifteen years,

you stumble upon one of the tapes. You are
surrounded by boxes, a lone black spot
beneath clear-eyed London skies – a rare thing.
Batteries located, you insert modern ear buds

into a pale blue SONY Walkman and press
play. Lionel Hampton's vibes ring out sharp
and cheery on "How High the Moon". Time drags
you back to your book-filled living room in Accra
where all your loves were seeded. You remember

what it feels like to be in love because it is right,
not because it's what's expected; you are lost,
close to heaven for 3.20 minutes before Hamp's
flourish pulls you to the present. As the sound
fades, a shadow falls over you. It may be
a passing bird, it may be the shape of your father's
silhouette. What is certain is a new song is
beginning, something with brushes as gentle
as lashes – and your cheeks are wet.

CASABLANCA

Prelude
Barely through with the opening credits, film music,
and already I'm mad; that projected map
that stuffs nations into someone else's dwarf
of an imagination: an entire history named French
West Africa, a bright inheritance of diamonds
and pain flagged for Leopold as Belgian
Congo. I'm relieved that the text inked over
the part of the continent I call home's blurred
so I can't see the insult. Then the Black man
from the United States of America starts playing
the white and black of the piano with a big smile.

Act One
Of my father's stories, the one with the Moroccan Amazigh
who taught him to shoot in London, has everything: star-
crossed lovers, adventure, a kind of betrayal. Shape-shifting
from speeches in the Black Power underworld, it was natural,
after attempts on his life and two sweet honey traps,
to head from Algiers, train and fight with the Independence
movements gaining traction in South West Africa. He broke up
with Kirsten, his Swedish lover, seen with him at a café
table in a picture in our house, staring at him
his whole life. Franz Fanon was waiting; he loved her
but he couldn't live at ease, knowing his people were not free.

Transition
[*Pan shot of expected desert scenes; rapid montage
of volunteers in training (remember Black people
can't be on screen for too long), flash quick image*

of Cuban flag as the new recruits take cover
behind sand dunes (maybe a hammer and sickle
for good measure), we hear a quick volley of gunfire,

fade to black present] In the last throes
of pre-militant partying, my father spotted
the shape of my mother across a room.

He raised his arm, the light was right; in autumn
night, a shadow fell, time goes by.

Act Two
Unlike the other darkies, he gets a speaking part; indeed
he's the soundtrack of *Rick's*, he moves with the man
from Paris to Casablanca – damn his private life, his needs
his desires, his family, the wo/man he loves. I see
how the lines are drawn: his piano can hold the transit
papers, but there is no transition for him. He plays
the tune, but he can't dance. If you don't know
the story, star-crossed lovers from Paris meet again
in Casablanca; there is a war on, stakes are high.
One lover, a bar owner (where the Black man plays)
sacrifices his feelings – we hope – for the greater good.

Act Three
In Kirsten's story, I guess I'd be part of the greater
good, except that she doesn't know my father never made it
to Algeria. She returned to Stockholm; she may have
had his picture, may have presumed him dead before cancer
took him – forever a hero in the frame of her memory.
Still, he was what she imagined – so full of love
with a capacity for the ruthless – as Mr Toft, spouse of
the Danish Consul found when he leered at my mother
likening her to coffee. My father gave him a 10-count, calmly

walked indoors to fetch the sturdy pistol he still had
a licence for from the 1960s – something from a Moroccan.

Closing Credits
The man (Mr Toft), given his belly, ran faster
than I've ever seen since, across the map of Africa,
earth beneath his feet. He may be in Brazzaville now
(a place of deceit and loss), with Renault and Rick.

VOGUE

Some nights my sleep is vain, wants
to watch itself in mirrors, show off
its twists, its feints, its hilarious ability

to evade capture, how it dips its toes in
blue daydreams, then runs past desperate hours,
its compass north and awake, to the edge of

faded moon bliss – a cliff over which it just hangs
its legs, like kids in chairs too high for them,
singing questions into the altitude of my stillness

like a random herd of nuns or Von Trapps ambushed
by Alps green. It turns to its good left side
to watch itself twerk, checks out its abs

from the front, contemplates a Periscope® stream
by the backlight of an Android®. I've tried
everything sensible adults do to drift off – yes,

ev . ery . thing. I've had to go back to being a boy,
up in that bunk bed, chattering wild dreams down
to my brother until we wake up in the morning

astonished that we slept – like when I'm in love,
whispering across pillows. Some nights my sleep wants
company and it won't settle its vogueing self for less.

11-Page Letter to (A)nyemi (A)kpa

I have the peculiar, but not rare background of having heritage both from the diaspora (the African people who were taken from their lands and made to labour unpaid in the Americas and the Caribbean) and the remaining inhabitants of the continent of Africa. As a result of that I carry an English surname in addition to my Ga names. As a result of that, my engagement with the world has always been in a minimum of two languages – one of which has always sought to belittle me. When I chose the name *11-Page Letter to (A)nyemi (A)kpa* as the title of this sequence, I was consciously shifting the frame of reference to my first language of love while retaining a link to my first language of oppression. Anyemi in Ga has *sibling* as its closest equivalent in English, but, since we don't have a separate word for *cousins* in Ga, it goes beyond *sibling* and – importantly – it is not gendered. Akpa means good – and it was such a joy to me that in coining a Ga compound word that would have the same abbreviation as 'African-American', I arrived at good sibling/cousin/fam. Our languages will always raise us to the level we deserve. I truly wanted to pay homage to Aaliyah at some point, but a *4-Page Letter* was not enough and I also wanted the visual effect of two siblings standing side-by-side that 11 gives, as well as the mathematical resolution of one-two-one that shifts number into the language of conversation. I wanted to write this poem as a start of the conversation that we should be having amongst ourselves as continent and diaspora – away from all the distraction we have been taught as knowledge in languages that are not our own. I want us to talk about the wound of being taken away as well as the wound of being left behind and wondering if your abducted family will ever return – the silent trauma that many African communities carry that are reflected in taboos and social codes that we haven't even began to unpack. As a child I never understood why I wasn't supposed to whistle when the sun began to set until I found out as an adult that at the height of the slave trade people were kidnapped by mercenaries if they were not quiet. I also want us to talk about the things we have kept in spite of all that was taken from us; how the most affecting compliment we retain across centuries, seas and loss is naa bo, i'na bo ei, wo nono... 'there you are', 'I see you'. How heartbreaking it is for us to be – in so many places – the invisible! This is a poem to say I see you.

Crossroad vs Blues
My late father raised me with a love for blues and one of the first CDs I bought was an 18-track John Lee Hooker album called *Boogie Man* from a UK blues magazine in 1994. I only owned 7 CDs at the time so I listened religiously and read all I could about the man. Summary? Illiterate, but a prolific lyricist – a perfect metaphor for oral styles of learning, history and growth. If proof were needed of his intelligence, he recognised how the record industry was exploiting Black musicians and signed contracts under different names to maximise his upfront recording income. Hooker's playing style was so idiosyncratic that it was hard to pull in a backing band for him so he tapped his own foot to accompany his songs. His story never left me and as I read about more blues musicians – male and female – I was stunned by how hard they had to fight to earn what they were worth. Even worse, the (mainly) British musicians who later came to imitate them became rich overnight. Suddenly, the Robert Johnson myth of selling his soul to the devil at a crossroad in order to gain his incredible virtuosic gift didn't sound like such a romantic idea after all. It sounded like erasure. These imitators, blessed with the means to buy guitars from early on, spend hours trying to master Johnson's sound and, when they couldn't, we start to hear about deals with the devil. It's a story that doesn't take into account the fact that Robert Johnson was ridiculed on stage early in his playing career, went away with the fire and fury of rejection and forged a sound that could no longer be ignored. It's a similar story with Black musicians in general; their brilliance is linked to struggle, with no explanation for how every other Black person is not an amazing musician. No, these blues artists are geniuses who make the complex appear simple, who achieve greatness in spite of oppression and struggle and they deserve respect. If the song seems simple, play it again.

ACKNOWLEDGEMENTS

For previously published poems:

Cordite Poetry Review for "Seeing Eyes"; *Miracle Monacle* for "Defences" and a section of "Caress", *Obsidian* for "Locking Doors"; *The Rialto* for "Trumpet"; *Johannesburg Review of Books* for "Bottle" and "Tree of the Invisible Man".

Thanks for the friends who see me, the family who hold me and the Ga language that gave me my foundation in dreaming.

ABOUT THE AUTHOR

Nii Ayikwei Parkes is a writer, editor and publisher, who has won acclaim as a children's author, poet, broadcaster and novelist. He is the author of the poetry chapbooks: *eyes of a boy, lips of a man* (1999), his début; *M is for Madrigal* (2004), a selection of seven jazz poems; and *Ballast* (2009), an imagination of the slave trade by balloon. His poem, 'Tin Roof', was selected for the Poems on the Underground initiative in 2007, followed by the poem 'Barter,' chosen from his first full collection *The Makings of You*, published by Peepal Tree in 2010. His novel, *Tail of the Blue Bird* (Jonathan Cape, 2009), hailed by the *Financial Times* as 'a beautifully written fable... simple in form, but grappling with urgent issues,' was lauded internationally, becoming a bestseller in Germany and notably winning France's two major prizes for translated fiction – Prix Baudelaire and Prix Laure Bataillon – in 2014. He is the author of two books for children under the name K.P. Kojo and has a collection of short stories, *The City Will Love You*, due from Unbound. Nii is the Senior Editor and publisher at flipped eye publishing, serves on the boards of World Literature Today and the AKO Caine Prize and produces the Literature and Talks programme at Brighton Festival.

As a socio-cultural commentator and advocate for African writing, Nii has led forums internationally, has sat on discussion panels for BBC Radio, and he founded the African Writers' Evening series.

ALSO BY NII AYIKWEI PARKES

The Makings of You
ISBN: 9781845231590; pp. 80; pub. 2010; £8.99

Nii Ayikwei Parkes' début collection encompasses the story of a triangular trade in reverse – a family history that goes from the Caribbean back to Sierra Leone, and in his own life from London to Ghana, and back again.

His gift as a poet is for the most rewarding kind of story-telling, including those stories told with wit and an engaging ambivalence about himself. His narratives move unerringly to a perfect punch-line, but in the collection as a whole there is a refreshing lack of complacency in his willingness to move out of his comfort zone and explore areas of imaginative fantasy, as in his 'Ballast' series, a *tour de force* of defamiliarisation, where he imagines how the slave trade would have gone had its mode of transport been the hot air balloon, rather than the slave ship.

There is much humour, but it comes from a family tradition of knowing that 'our jokes weren't really funny, they were just sad/ stories we learned to laugh at'. Like all poets with a largeness of heart, with no embarrassment about embracing the deepest feelings, Parkes has an especial sensitivity to the promise and acute sensitivities of childhood, both his own and others'.